MONSTER

MONSTER

DANIEL MacIVOR
DANIEL BROOKS

Monster
first published 1999 by
Scirocco Drama
An imprint of J. Gordon Shillingford Publishing Inc.
© 1999 Daniel MacIvor and Daniel Brooks

Scirocco Drama Series Editor: Dave Carley
Cover illustration by Lisa Kiss
Cover design by Terry Gallagher/Doowah Design Inc.
Author photo by Guntar Kravis
Printed and bound in Canada

We acknowledge the support of The Canada Council for the Arts and the
Manitoba Arts Council for our publishing program.

Canadian Cataloguing in Publication Data

MacIvor, Daniel, 1962–
Monster

A play.
ISBN 1-896239-55-2

    I. Brooks, Daniel, 1958- II. Title.

PS8575.I86M66 1999   C812'.54   C99-901088-3
PR9199.3.M33M66 1999

For Buster, Emma and Kate

Daniel Brooks and Daniel MacIvor

About the Authors

Daniel MacIvor has been creating theatre since 1986. He is a writer, performer, director, producer and artistic director of da da kamera. His plays include *See Bob Run, Wild Abandon, Never Swim Alone, 2-2 Tango, House, Here Lies Henry* and *The Soldier Dreams*. His plays have toured extensively throughout Canada, the United States, Israel, the United Kingdom, and Australia.

Daniel Brooks is an accomplished director, writer, actor, and teacher, considered to be at the forefront of Canada's new generation of theatre artists. Co-artistic director of da da kamera and founder of the Augusta Company, he is a recipient of the Pauline McGibbon award for outstanding direction, the Edinburgh Fringe First award, two Chalmers awards for new Canadian plays and three Dora Mavor Moore awards.

Production Credits

Monster was originally produced by da da kamera and premiered at Canadian Stage Company, Toronto, on April 21, 1998, starring Daniel MacIvor.

Created by Daniel MacIvor and Daniel Brooks
Sound and Music Composed by Richard Feren
Lighting Design: Andy Moro and Daniel Brooks
Technical Director: Andy Moro
Associate Artist: Sarah Phillips
Produced by Sherrie Johnson
Development Partners: Festival Antigonish, Antigonish,NS; High Performance Rodeo, Calgary, AB; Theatre Project, Baltimore, MD; Canadian Stage Company, Toronto, ON

Characters

Monster is a one man show.

Staging

In the original production, *Monster* was performed without costume changes or props (save for a glass filled with liquid which Joe picks up off stage, drinks, then casts aside). This movement off stage was the only moment the performer moved from his centre spot.

MONSTER

(Black. Long pause.)

ADAM: *(Whispering.)* Shh. Asshole.
The movie's starting. You don't want to miss the movie. Everybody loves the movies. And the movie begins with the beginning of time. With darkness and silence. The darkness before the first dawn, where nature is yet a fetus of the mother it will be; where there are no saints because there are no sinners to need saints. Dark and silent. And the silence is broken by the whispering voice. The whispering voice from the darkness. The whispering voice from the darkness which says: "Shh Asshole. The movie's starting." And from the darkness...
And from the darkness...
And from the darkness come...I.

(Music. Light slowly up.)

Come I. Come I. Come Me. Come Mine. Come My. Come I. Come I.
Come I. Come I. Come Me. Come Mine. Come My. Come I. Come I.
Come I. Come I. Come Me. Come Mine. Come My. Come I. Come I.
I'd rather be an ocean to a drowning man than a drink to a man in the desert.
I'd rather be a fire to a forest than a fire to a forty day blizzard.
I'd rather be a flood to a village of ten than a dam to a nation of millions.

I'd rather be a blackout than a burst of light, a very short day and a very long night.
Mine will be mine, mine will be all, mine be my only concern.
Mine will be mine, mine will be all, mine be my only concern.
Mine will be mine, mine will be all, mine be my only concern.
And you wonder:
Who is this guy?
Why am I here?
What's in it for me?
What's In It For…ME.

(*Light shift.*)

ADAM: Good morning.

JANINE: Good morning.

AL: Morning.

JANINE: Did you sleep well?

AL: (*Sarcastically.*) Yeah great.

JANINE: Are you being sarcastic?

AL: Aw I had that nightmare again.

JANINE: Which nightmare?

AL: (*Angry.*) Jesus Janine, the same nightmare I always have!

JANINE: Well thank you very much, that's a nice way to start the day!

AL: I'm sorry, it's not you it's me.

JANINE: It certainly is!

AL: I'm sorry.

JANINE: Well, which nightmare?

AL: The one where I'm running down the street naked covered in blood and screaming.

JANINE: Oh, the one about your Dad.

AL: Yeah the one about my Dad.

JANINE: Well you know what honey? Al? Honey?

AL: *(Shaving.)* What?

JANINE: *(Putting on her bra.)* You know what you should do next time you have that nightmare? You should just turn around and face whatever it is you're running away from and just say: Stop!

AL: Christ Janine you're such a simp.

JANINE: What?

AL: Nothing. Yeah thanks I'll try it. Thanks.

JANINE: What?

AL: NOTHING!

               (Light shift.)

ADAM: Al! Now now Al there's no reason to be angry at Janine. It's not Janine's fault you're in a bad mood. That's Al and Janine. You'll be seeing more of them later. They fight like that all the time. And if it's like that now what's it going to be like when they get married. If they even get that far. But something tells me that they will. I guess that's love talking. And she has a point though. I mean if you're having a nightmare who's going to step in for you? Seems to me it's up to you. To step in and stop it. Stop!
I think it's a good idea.
Stop!
I might try it myself sometime. If I ever have a nightmare.
Stop.

But that would take discipline. To step in and stop it. Discipline. And that's in short supply these days. Well between absent parents and child-centered-child rearing there's no discipline. So what happens? The kids run wild. Or they sit around on their cans all day doing nothing.
"There's nothing to do. There's nothing to do."
Read a book. Clean your room.
"There's nothing to do."
Say your prayers!

(Light and sound.)

MONTY: There's nothing to do.
There's nothing to do.
Nothing ever happens. Here. To me. Whatever.
Except for last summer.
Whoa. That was something that happened. That was something that really happened. It didn't really happen to me though, but it happened to the neighbourhood, it happened to the city, it happened to the world, it was in all the papers, you probably even read about it even. Remember last summer? The weather was so weird—maybe that's why it happened. Last summer, remember, where they played that lame song on the radio all the time and everybody was doing that lame dance to it? They said it was cool but no cool people were into it. Only old farts and little freaks were into it. Lame. July first. I know because that's when my Mom always has her incredibly lame barbecue for like stinky old Great Uncle Ernie and all the inbred little cousins. You know, the kind of barbecue where they're always coming up to you and asking "What grade are you in?" Which is so interesting to talk about like in the summer. Right. But it was while we were having the barbecue that it happened. No well I mean no I mean the whole torture thing was happening all weekend—and it was a long weekend so it was three days of torture.

But it was while we were having the barbecue that they found the body.

(Sound.)

Apparently what happened was the two cops went down into the basement and it was really dark and the first thing they could make out was this big cardboard box in the middle of the room all soggy on the bottom and then an old record player with a record on it going round and round and round and behind the record player the furnace and behind the furnace the cot and on the cot there was this thing but they couldn't make out what it was. And then in the darkness they hear "Why?" And that's when they turn on the light. And that's when they see what's in the box, and that's when they see what's on the cot. And what's on the cot was a head and a torso and what's in the box was everything else.
One cop barfed in our backyard. The other cop had to take early retirement.

Raindrops Keep Falling on Your Head. Or whatever. Which is apparently some old song from some movie. That was the record on the stereo.

They Were So Weird.
I mean I should know right because they lived right next door. And they were. So weird. I mean even their name right. Boyle. Think about it. Boil. Which maybe if you were cool you might be able to get away with a name like that but if you are weird and have a name like that then that makes you weirder. I mean there are lots of weird names like this guy I know Steve Fleck which becomes Flecker which becomes Pecker Flecker which becomes Jerk Off which becomes Jerk and that's pretty misfortunate; but the Boyles, they were weird. Especially B-Boy. That's what we called him. B-Boy. We used to call him Boyle Boy but Boyle

Boy was too hard to say especially if you were chasing him and yelling you know: "Get back here Boyle Boy so I can kick your head in!" Not that I ever said that or whatever. But it was easier to say "Get back here B-Boy so I can give you...um... something nice..." or you know.

He was so weird.

That kid couldn't even ride a bike. And he smelled like Irish Spring soap all the time because he used way too much of it, like he put six bars under each armpit. And he picked his nose. Till it bled. I know, I saw it. And Mister Boyle he was weird too. He coached soccer. Need I say more. And he drank. A lot. But I guess I mean like whose dad doesn't right. Unless you're in the Salvation Army or the Mormons. But when my dad used to live here, whoa, our fridge was like: you open up the fridge and it's like some kind of beer store, like there's like a line up of people in there and some guy behind the milk carton like: "Hey can I help you?" And this other guy: "Ya gimme a six-pack of everything." Hey guy, that's my fridge okay? They don't drink in the Salvation Army or the Mormons though, I know because I had this Big Brother one time who was in the Salvation Army, he didn't drink he played the trumpet, would've been cooler if he played the guitar. But he didn't. He moved to the west coast though because he was stalking a Mormon.

And Mrs B, she was weird too, because she was really high strung—that's what my Mom said, because she was always trying to be overachieving as the perfect Mom, so she was always acting like Moms on detergent commercials and so she was always carrying this tray out into the back yard with stuff or whatever on it. Like in the summertime it would be like of lemonade and cookies—or in the winter time it would be like of hot chocolate and mini-marshmallows—but she was always doing this carrying-a-tray-out-into-the-backyard thing. Which was really sad because there was never anybody in the backyard. Except B-Boy. Or maybe me if I was you know desperate or grounded or something. But she was so weird she didn't even notice how sad it was.

I ate there once.
I was just trying to be nice. You know what they had for dinner? Spaghetti. Just spaghetti. And I don't mean just spaghetti just spaghetti I mean just spaghetti period. Plain spaghetti. Like with nothing on it. Like not even cheese. Like not even catsup. Like not even shaking cheese. Naked spaghetti. And—even weirder... Mrs B cut up Mister Boyle and B-Boy's spaghetti for them. Like right in front of me. And they didn't even try to stop her out of shame or anything. Like if she'd come up to me to cut up my spaghetti I'd be like: "Back off Lady! That's too weird!" But she didn't.
I mean they were truly deeply weird but I still don't think he should have had to die like that.
I mean like I said he coached soccer right, I mean, okay, he never coached me but I mean I've been coached, I've been to out of town tournaments okay, I've stayed in hotels okay, I know what goes on. Like midnight like, knock knock knock, like "How's your sore leg?" like knock knock knock, like "Why don't I rub your sore leg?" like "Relax while I rub your sore leg." Like that's not my leg Mister Boone? Why don't you try Steve Fleck down the hall? Tssss, I hate when that happens.
And he beat her. Mister Boyle did. Beat Mrs B. That's what my Mom said—because one time my mom saw Mrs B at Craft Club and she had a black eye and my Mom asked her what happened and Mrs B said "Oh nothing I just fell down" —Like what? Into a doorknob? And Mrs B was always going to stay at her mom's or her sister's place or something, like all unexpectedly, like in the middle of the night? Which is apparently a sure-fire sign.

And she was staying at her mom's or her sister's place or something the weekend it happened. And when she came back and saw what happened she was totally freaked out. Totally freaked out. And I think she was probably partly totally freaked out out of guilt; because she wished she'd done it. That's projection. It's psychological. It's where you have these really intense feelings for this person or this thing and you can't handle it so you put it on some other person or thing but sometimes it can backfire and you have a complete mental breakdown and have to go on perscription drugs and then you walk funny cause your feet feel swollen. It happens to people.
But I guess I mean she would have just cause to be totally freaked out because what happened was so totally weird.

(Sound.)

Apparently what happened was B-Boy gets Mister Boyle down into the basement under false pretences like he says: Come on down the basement Dad I taught the dog a trick or… No they didn't have a dog… Or, come down down to the basement Dad I fixed the stereo… Like he would've believed that… Or Hey Dad there's beer down here. And then Mister Boyle goes down and he's like "Okay where's the beer" and then B-Boy throws this fishing net over Mister Boyle and then whacks him on the head with this canoe oar and when Mister Boyle comes to he's all tied up to the cot behind the furnace behind the stereo and he's like "What the hell's going on" or whatever like "You are so dead" and there's B-Boy and he turns around and he's holding this hacksaw. This hacksaw from this tool set which was given by Mrs B to Mister Boyle and B-Boy the Christmas before as a joint present so they could bond. Bond. She even used the word 'bond'. You can read it. It was in the paper. I cut it out. It's in my scrapbook. And he's standing there with this hacksaw, still with the ribbon on it and Mister Boyle's like "What the hell's going on?" Like "You are so dead" like not getting it, and with the hacksaw he cuts off Mister Boyle's finger from the tip of the finger to the second joint, just like that, and then, he takes this blowtorch and with this blow torch he uses it to cauterise the wound to stop the bleeding—which he saw on this weird science show on cable— which we all saw right—you only needed cable to see it—they talk about violence on television what about science on television. And then he cuts from the second joint to the knuckle and then each finger like that in two pieces and then the thumbs and the hands and the forearms and the humerises and the everything until Mister Boyle is just a head and a torso. A living head and torso. A living head and torso which B-Boy forces to watch over the course of the whole long weekend while B-Boy takes each piece of Mister Boyle and puts it in this cardboard box which on one side has written on it: 'Apology' and on the other side has printed on it: 'Some Assembly Required'.

Would that not make a fantastic movie?

(Light and sound.)

(Scream.) "For god's sake what are you doing, stop please stop!"

"No! Are you sorry now? Are you? Are you sorry for that finger that pointed out all my mistakes, are you sorry for that thumb that never said things would be okay, are you sorry for that hand that never helped me up?"

"Yes I'm sorry, now stop this please, I'm your father."

"You might be my father but I am the son. I am the son created to destroy you!!"

(Light and sound restored.)

...or whatever.

Raindrops Keep Falling on Your Head.

That was the record that B-Boy played over and over on the stereo to drown out the screams of Mister Boyle. Which is true because my Mom remembers remembering hearing it when she went to light the barbecue...

And weirdest: he fed him. B-Boy fed Mister Boyle. And he didn't have to right, it was only three days, like you can live like thirty days or sixty days or something without eating. But he did. He fed him. Spaghetti. Plain Spaghetti. And you can imagine Mister Boyle on the cot just a head and a torso and maybe a bit of a thigh and B-Boy all crouched down beside him cutting up the spaghetti just like Mrs B. would have done and feeding it to his Dad. "Here have some spaghetti."

Have some spaghetti!

And I think that proves that B-Boy really loved his dad. Or...not...

Imagine what a drag it would be to have plain spaghetti as your last meal.

Imagine if that happened to you.

(Sound and light.)

ADAM: What a great kid. It's such a shame what happened to him. You see he became so obsessed with that crime he could think about nothing else. He set up a mock-up of the crime scene in his own basement; he became fixated on all the details: the weight of the body parts in the cardboard box, the amount of blood lost between the incision and the cauterisation. He went to the library every day and pored over medical texts, over all the old newspaper articles about the crime, he made multiple photocopies, he had five identical scrapbooks. He could think about nothing else he could talk about nothing else. But people stopped wanting to talk about that because better things happened: those teenaged girls in Wisconsin who ate their grandmother, the woman in Niagara Falls who made jewellery out of her baby's bones and sold it to tourists. But this poor kid was only interested in the Boyles and B-Boy and why did B-Boy do it. Why? And that's the question that pushed that poor kid so far inside himself that he was lost in a world of why's. And why is the question that we're left with when we ask why did that poor kid do what he did. One night. Took a long walk. Out along the highway. Until he got to the most treacherous spot. And he stood there. And he waited.

(Sound and light as MONTY walks into traffic.)

ADAM: "Why…"

(Light and sound restored.)

Poor kid.
But everybody's got their story. I know you do. And you know I do. That's why you're here. And I'm very glad you are. It's nice to see you. Of course you're all older and uglier and stupider than you were twenty minutes ago—but that's no crime. Well what do you expect, what with your hectic schedule and accomplishing nothing all day. *(Pause.)* I said what with your hectic schedule and accomplishing nothing all day. *(Pause.)* Hmm, I thought that was pretty funny when I thought of it. But I guess I'm no comedian… Oh. Hey. Somebody here doesn't like me. Well that better stop or you'll be ejected. Or worse I'll get you up here and explain to everybody how you've manipulated every situation you've ever been involved in so that it would benefit yourself. Yes I'm talking to you asshole.
No I wouldn't do that! I'm just joshing ya! Don't be scared. What have you got to be scared of? You're the King. Yes you are the King of your world. Each

of you is. The King or Queen of your world. So what you Kings and Queens want to do is line your fears up against the wall and call the firing squad. There's some good advice.

Hi. I'm Adam. You can call me Adam.

(Sound: "Hi Adam.")

Fuck off! Oooo! I hate that name. Well hate is strong, after all it is the name that will be chosen for me and it certainly does have its significance, its history; but you see that's just it, because History doesn't appeal to me because History doesn't apply to me because I don't actually exist.
Ah, me me me me me, enough about him. Let's talk about someone else, let's talk about someone who does exist. Let's talk about Al.

(Sound: phone ring, voice: "Janine on two.")

AL: Hello.

JANINE: Hi honey, it's Janine.

AL: Yes Janine, I know it's Janine that's why we pay a receptionist to tell me it's Janine.

JANINE: You think you're being funny but you're not you're being mean.

AL: I'm sorry. What is it?

JANINE: I was thinking—

AL: Uh huh.

JANINE: I think I know what your nightmare's about.

AL: Janine I'm at work.

JANINE: I know but tonight.

AL: I have my meeting tonight.

JANINE:	I know but after your meeting.
AL:	No Janine honey I'm going to stay at my place tonight.
JANINE:	No you're just going to go home and get all grumpy.
AL:	I just need to spend some time on my own.
JANINE:	You can spend some time on your own with me.
AL:	Not tonight Janine.
JANINE:	Yes you owe me a movie, you said!
AL:	Not tonight.
JANINE:	You owe me a movie!
AL:	Not —
JANINE:	You owe me a movie you owe me a movie you owe me—
AL:	All right all right all right!

(Light restored.)

ADAM: Al! Settle down! What a hothead. If you don't want to do it just say no. "All right all right all right." Who's the simp now? But we should not judge Al too harshly too quickly because as da Vinci said: "One does not have the right to dislike a thing that one does not fully understand." And if da Vinci said that it must be true because he was smart. And so in the spirit of da Vinci, in the spirit of smartness, in order that we might more fully understand Al we're going to take a trip. Back in time—back before the summer of love, back when Vietnam was just a place on a map, back around the time Marilyn went to sleep, two weeks before Al gets his first tooth. And we're going to meet: Al's dad.

(Light and sound.)

AL'S DAD: Rob Roy, Rob Roy, Manhattan, Rob Roy, Creme de
              menthe
              Rob Roy, Rob Roy, Manhattan, Rob Roy, Creme de
              menthe

              (Baby cries.)

              Rob Roy, Rob Roy, Manhattan, Rob Roy,

              (Baby cries.)

              HELEN!

ADAM: That's Al's Dad. He's in his living room having a
              few drinks on a Saturday afternoon. And there's
              nothing wrong with that. He built this house, he's
              made this life for his family, there's nothing wrong
              with a guy having a few drinks in his living room
              on a Saturday afternoon.

AL'S DAD: Rob Roy, Rob Roy, Manhattan,

              (Baby cries.)

              Rob Roy, Margarita, HELEN!

ADAM: —is Al's Dad's wife. Al's mom. She's in the garden
              out back. She spends a lot of time in the garden. She
              almost never takes off her gardening gloves. Oh!
              Maybe that's why Al brought Janine those
              gardening gloves that night and asked her to wear
              them while she… Oh but you don't need to know
              the dirty details do ya? Anyway:

              (Baby continues to cry.)

AL'S DAD: Rob Roy, Rob Roy, Manhattan, Rob Roy, Margarita
              Rob Roy, Rob Roy—
              Why won't that baby stop crying?

ADAM: —in the next room, that's little Al.

AL'S DAD: Rob Roy, Rob Roy, Manhattan, Rob Roy, Zambucca.
Rob Roy, Rob Roy, Manhattan—
Why won't that baby stop crying?

ADAM: The baby won't stop crying Mister Al's Dad because he's just like you. He can feel everything. And you know how bad it can feel to feel everything. That's why you're so fond of your:

AL'S DAD: Rob Roy, Manhattan, Zambucca, Rob Roy, Martini, Creme de menthe
WHY WON'T THAT BABY STOP CRY—!

(ADAM throttles AL's DAD, silencing him.)

ADAM: Because he can feel everything.
See that happens to some people. Some people have flat feet, some people have bad backs, some people get headaches, some people have allergies and some people can feeling everything. I've got that. I can feel what you're feeling. It's not like I can read your minds or anything like— Well it's not like I can read everybody's mind, but there's always a few... Okay, now I don't want to single anyone out and I don't want to turn into the Amazing Kreskin here but somebody in the room is concerned about their daughter and I just want to say that well...it's a tough one...especially in this case, but... I'll just say that all your concern and all your worry isn't going to change a thing, she's just going to end up hating you anyway so why don't you just forget about it and have some fun.
See. I can feel things. But so can you. That's why you're here. Shhhh!
The movie's starting:

(Light shift.)

JOE: Hello my name is Joe and I'm an addict.
Which is a good thing.

I mean it's not a good thing to be, you know what I'm saying, but it's a good thing to know.

And I know.

When I was using I was using everything. I'd drink, ingest, swallow, inhale anything—except paint thinner because one time paint thinner almost made me go temporarily blind.

Since I was fourteen the longest I'd ever been clean before this stretch was forty-eight hours and that was because I was having my appendix out and my dealer couldn't find the hospital. This time I decided to get sober partly because of the fact that one of my kidneys broke on through to the other side and partly because of the fact that I realized that when you're down there in the dirt, in the mud, in the shit—all anybody down there cares about is themselves and screw you and what's in it for me and that's not where I wanted to be anymore, you know what I'm saying. So I quit everything.

Problem was once I quit everything I'd wake up every morning and not know what to do, you know what I'm saying, with myself. What, you know, should I, you know, do? My girlfriend Pam said that was just how it felt to be normal and that I'd get used to it. Course my getting used to it that would be wishful thinking on Pam's part because ever since I cleaned up I haven't been able to—well I've been able to—but—I can't seem to—with Pam—it's—just—I don't know—my heart's not in it. Course Pam says "It's not your heart I need in it." Pam's great. So. I didn't know what to do so I would just you know do nothing and wait. For something to happen. But man you can wait and you can wait. There's me every morning: looking out my dirty window: schoolbuses pass, churchbells chime, ladies in new shoes, guys in ties with briefcases in elevators, the enormous world passing me by, Pam not getting any and me doing nothing. So I figure it's up to me to, you know, step into my own life, and you know what I'm saying, make something happen. So I try to, you know, do a few things, you know, get in touch with my old man and try to reconnect with him, I do a few, you know, fix up things around the place and that and I call into a few of those phone-in radio shows. But see I saw I needed something bigger something I could really put myself into something I mean something with a payoff that maybe was going to change my life. Something huge see. So this one night I go to bed, and listen I'm not the kind of guy who prays okay but sometimes I do and when I do I say "Is anybody out there?" and then I say my you know petition or my thing. So this one night I go to bed and I say "Is anybody out there?" and I say "Could I please have something to, you know what I'm saying, do?" Well the next morning I wake up and honest to, you know, whatever, there it is. In my head like a gift. This one perfectly formed idea. Which is a movie. Now I don't mean an idea for a movie I mean a whole entire, you know what I'm saying, movie. I mean this is like if you could plug a cable into my head and connect it to a screen it would play this whole entire movie from credits to credits just like that. I mean excuse my French but: fuck me blind and call me Friday! Where'd that come from?

And it's good. I mean it's the kind of thing you've got to see but I'll try I mean I'm not really a verbal type of guy but well stuff—I mean some stuff is like the beginning where it's all quiet and dark and you wonder has it started yet and all of a sudden it has and then it's the hero. Gary Oldman! Gary Oldman! Now there is a man who's been there, you know what I'm saying, there is a man who knows! And it's an on the run type of story and he's on the run and then he meets up with this beautiful mysterious hitchhiker who is in my head played in some scenes by Yasmine Bleeth and in some scenes by Uma Thurman—which is, you know, very

interesting to, you know, have two people be one person because hey aren't we all at least two or more people at least, you know what I'm saying— and when he and her first meet they talk and they realize they met once before years ago in this bookstore in Baltimore and he says "Small world" and she says "No it's not" and he says "It's not?" and she says "Not if you have to go up to each and every person who deserves it and kick their ass." Then it's a love story. And they're on the run and they're in love and they hook up with this friendly dwarf who becomes their buddy and gets them out of all these tight corners they end up getting themselves in and then this one really nice scene late at night on the beach and the friendly dwarf looks at Gary Oldman and the friendly dwarf says "You're on your own man" and then the friendly dwarf explodes. And you're on your own is a kind of recurring kind of motif all through the um, you know what I'm saying… And this great scene later where Gary Oldman is despondent because his buddy the friendly dwarf is gone and because Uma and Yasmine end up meeting and running off together on him and he is standing at the edge of the highway and he realizes the only way he can heal the sadness of the world is to "end it all" and so he steps out into the oncoming traffic but just when he does the highway turns into a river and the cars all turn into fish and Gary Oldman walks safely through the river of the highway to the other side. It's a miracle. Oh yeah and then the last scene which is kind of strange kind of dreamy and it's Gary Oldman but as a kid and he's in the basement with his old man and he's got this hacksaw and he cuts his old man up into little pieces with this hacksaw and puts all the pieces in this cardboard box while *Raindrops Keep Falling on My Head* keeps playing over and over on repeat on the CD…on repeat on CD…on repeat on CD.
Credits. The end.

Yeah. Well. It's not *Schindler's List* but, you know, it's not to everybody's taste but what is? But I'm telling you it's one hundred and seventy percent better than most of the crap that's out there. But it doesn't matter anyway if you like it or not because it's my thing. It's my thing that I've got to do with my life. And I know what you're thinking. "Oh yeah this guy make a movie, yeah right." But you know what, you could probably write a letter to Steven Speilberg tomorrow and tell him how he should make a movie of your grandmother's life because one time she helped her blind neighbour paint his fence and he just might. Because that's how it works. The idea could be as dumb as anything but you've just got to take the initiative. See you're thinking that movies are all glamorous and big stars and trailers full of money but it's not all like that at all. It's actually pretty regular most of it. Probably more regular than working in an office. Making movies is, movies is...it's more like digging a ditch, or building a building—it's just your imagination and magazines that makes you think that its glamorous. And plus I happen to have some connections to the movie business from Pam from these guys she used to know from when she used to dance at the Wigwam. And this guy who knows this guy who knows who you know how it goes this guy Murray who's a producer. And Murray's like: "Hey how ya doing?" Like: "Hey how ya doing?" Murray; he's got one lung and half a larynx. And I meet Murray and I tell him my idea and Murray's like: "It's shit." And I'm like "Oh" and he's like: "But shit sells." And I'm like: "So what should I write it down or what?" And he's like: "No that's okay we got assholes we pay to do that kind of shit work. Aaron!" Aaron. Aaron. "Hey how are you doing? Hey how are you doing wassup?" Aaron. This guy he's a writer. "Hey how are you doing wassup? Lemme getya a drink?" He's Jewish but he's not stuck up about it or

anything and does he drink? Man I didn't know
they drank. But he drinks. "Lemme getya a drink.
Lemme getya a drink." No I don't drink. No I don't
drink. I've got to remind him every time. I go to his
place three times, these three nights and I'm telling
him all about the movie, you know I'm explaining
everything to him about the story; the characters:
what they say, what they do, what they wear, the
colour of the chairs the whole you know what I'm
saying thing and Denise is there taking notes who
is his girl, his assistant, his girl, and she's taking
notes and she's very nice except she's got this
"Excuse me I gotta pee" thing going on. "Excuse
me I gotta pee." and either she's got a bladder as
big as a nit or she's working on the worst coke habit
this side of Columbia. "Excuse me I gotta pee" Hey
what's going on man you just peed ten seconds
ago. "Ya I guess my bladder's as big as a..." Nit?
"Ya. Ha." Ya ha ha. But you know she's nice
enough and she's taking notes and we get to the
end of the movie and they say let's have a
champagne toast and you know what I'll say?
"You got any ginger ale?" They got champagne!
They got cocaine! I'm asking for ginger ale! Cause
now I've got my thing, my thing I'm going to do
with my life. So we get to the end, have a
champagne toast, ginger ale for me. Sign some
papers. I leave. And then—nothing. Okay. All this
time goes by. Nothing. I'm so excited and then
nothing and at first I'm thinking you know okay
maybe it didn't work out but that's okay cause
there's so many movie people in the world! You
could stand on any street corner in any city and
throw a rotten orange and you'd probably hit a
movie person or maybe okay maybe hey it is
working out it's just you have to have patience
with these things I mean it took thirty-five years or
something to make *Planet of the Apes*. But the
amazing thing is that all this time that nothing is
happening—everything is happening with me—

because I don't want a drink I don't want a snort I don't want a pill I don't want a hooker I don't want to be jealous of Pam because now I've got my thing. I've got my idea. I'm keeping a notebook, I'm going to the Y, I'm off dairy, I'm a different guy. Then. We get this call from Denise's girl inviting us to this premiere and I'm thinking okay sure do some networking, talk some movies, reconnect with these guys; so Pam and me we go and we get there, very tony affair, and we sit down and the movie starts and it's my movie! It's my movie. I mean it's not exactly... I mean some things are different: I mean Gary Oldman's not in it but it's this Gary Oldman type of guy but the friendly dwarf is there and the highway and the fish are there and the girlfriend's there, but there's only one person playing her but it is Yasmine Bleeth; but one thing they changed is they put the end at the beginning so that the kid and his old man in the basement is the thing the Gary Oldman type guy's on the run from which I guess makes more, you know what I'm saying, sense—in my idea it was more, you know what I'm saying, artistic. But whatever cause people seem to love it cause: get this: at the end? They all clap! Like a concert! And after there's a party.

(Sound.)

A party. A party that two years ago would have been my favourite kind of party because it has an open bar but I don't do that anymore, and everybody's got that I'm-so-interesting-I've-got-coke grin on but I don't do that anymore, and you can just smell how messed up everybody's planning to get later on but I don't do that anymore. And I'm on my own because Pam's at the bar looking for Yasmine Bleeth—suddenly she's a fan, and I'm pretty much on my own but that's okay because I know lots of people here. Murray, I saw him in a crowd of people and Aaron, he's pretty high I'm trying to stay away from him and Denise, she was at the door. Hey Murray! Murray! Hey over here!

—"Hey Joe how you doing? Did you like the picture?"

—I did I did I did I did I did I did sooooooo… when do I get my cheque.

—"Right right ha ha you're a funny guy just a second I'll grab us something from the bar."

—Hey No I don't drink… Hey…

—Hey Aaron? Aaron. How you doing?

—"Uh huh uh huh wassup Gordon"

—Joe.

—"Right Joe Man, hey so wassup? Lemme getya a drink."

—No! Hey So listen Aaron what's the deal on this picture, it's going to be playing around or what?

—"It's going to be huge hang on lemme get us something from the bar."

—No hey wait hey. Aaron! It was my idea man.

—"You stole it."

—Huh?

—"You stole that idea."

—Huh? Hey you're the dwarf from the movie.

—"Yeah now I'm the dwarf from the party. You stole that idea."

—No I didn't.

—"Yes you sure did, from Jerry Buster Foster."

—Who?

—"Jerry Buster Foster. *Yardstick Clothesline*? *Merry Xmas Santa's Dead*? *A Long Slow Death in August*? You never heard of Jerry Buster Foster?

—No.

—"Bullshit. This is his unfinished film *Hack*. I know I read the script."

—I think you're wrong.

—"I think you're an asshole."

—Cool down little guy.

—"Little guy? Little guy? You're dead faggot."
—It was my idea!

—"Could you keep it down please."
—Denise thank God, what the hell's going on with
my movie?
—"Your movie? It's Murray's movie."
—It was my idea.
—"Well what do you want you got a credit."
—What credit?
—"At the end. A special thanks."
—Special thanks?
—"Excuse me I gotta pee."
—It was my idea.
—"I'll mention it to Murray."
—Hey!
Hey. So it looks like I got ripped off but I guess you
got to start someplace. And I'm on my own.
Murray's nowhere to be seen, Aaron's out front
trying to flag a cab with two teenaged girls and a
tank of nitrous oxide, Denise has got herself
barricaded in the ladies room, Pam's probably
going down on Yasmine Bleeth's bodyguard by
now. And I'm on my own. And I feel so big and
strange and like I don't speak the right language
and everybody else looks great and has that
smooth easy lubricated 11:30-and-an-open-bar-
talk kind of talk going on. "Can I get you
something from the bar?" No thanks. "Can I get
you something from the bar?" No thanks! Then
Murray sends over a glass of champagne. I don't
drink. And Murray sends over a line of coke on
Uma Thurman's pussy. I don't do that man. And
Murray sends over the blood of Christ in a brand
new needle. I don't do that shit man! You ever see
a bird in a building? A bird trapped in a building—
and he thinks he's in a cage but he's not and there's
an easy way out but he can't find it cause he's so
freaked out? Well that's me. I'm the bird. I'm the
bird in the building. I just need a way out. I need a

day off. I need to forget. To obliterate. Pam?!
Sometimes a guy just needs to take a break. Who
am I trying to kid? I'm a party guy. I'm a late night
guy that's who I am. Who am is supposed to be if I
can't be myself?!

(JOE gets a glass of wine.)

You know last week I was helping my old man
move. He was moving out of his girlfriend's place
and into his own place. And I picked up this big
box that was really heavy and I said hey what's in
here and he says "Oh they're my golfing trophies."
I say your what? He says "My golfing trophies." I
didn't even know my old man golfed.

(JOE puts glass to lips.)

Well who am I supposed to be if I can't be myself?

(JOE drinks. He discards the glass. Light shift.)

It's the mists of Avalon. It's the fountains of
Atlantis. It's the fires of Rome. It's the showgirls of
Vegas. It's five minutes to midnight all night long
and I'm back!
And I'm out of there and someplace else,
someplace me! And it's elbows on the bar and a
lovely creature at the taps and she lives just
upstairs and what a wonderful record collection:
America, Bread, Crosby, Stills I love Neil Young
and there's beer in the fridge and whiskey in the jar
and hydro in a little wooden box on the coffee table
and lots more where that came from and ten
minutes later it's the bedroom and every pose of
the Kama Sutra and every wish of the bone, and
I'm not talking turkey and then she's spent but I'm
still ready, I'm still up, I'm still gone and I'm on the
street and down the alley with the boom boom
boom where the DJ spins pure noise all night long,
and there are no line ups in the can for all the lines
you can do, where every conversation fills you up

and you're so right and that's so true and you're so
smart and you're so funny and you're so pretty and
you're so strong and you're so red and that's so
blue and you're so me and I'm so you and we're so
us and go go go and the upstairs bar and the
downstairs lounge and the handjob in the back of
the yellow cab, thank you sister! to the windowless
backroom and the soda-can pipe that builds me a
monument, a monolith a mountain of midnight
and up up up the mountain I go until I'm at the top
where there's a view, a heavenly vista, an all round
view of you—of me! The way I should be! It's me
it's me I'm finally back I'm finally free! I am King of
my—! And then without warning gravity's gone.
And gravity does a lot. Gravity makes the stuff stay
in your stomach, gravity keeps your tongue from
sticking to the roof of your mouth, gravity lets your
eyes close from time to time. But now my eyes are
so wide open and I've got no circulation in my legs
and all my organs are in my chest and it doesn't
feel very good and I just want more but more's not
enough because nothing's enough because more's
just more and more's not enough. And Pam! I'm
sorry!... Then gravity's back with an angry
vengeance and down I come—back down to the
mud, to the dirt, to the shit, back where I belong.
And the sun comes up and the party's over and the
credits roll and I go home and Pam is gone and
where's the payoff and screw them and what the
hell's in it for me? (*Pause.*) Anyway. I guess today's
the first day of the rest of my blah blah blah.

Anyway. That's all. Thanks for listening. Thanks
all. Thanks for listening. Thanks. That's all.

(*Light shift.*)

RON: All right then, thank you Joe.

DAVID: Thanks Joe.

TINA: Thanks Joe.

AL: Thanks uh Joe.

RON: All right then would anyone else like to share?

DAVID: Yeah Ron. Hi my name is David and I'm an alcoholic.

RON: Hi David.

JOE: Hey David.

TINA: Hi David.

AL: Hi um David.

DAVID: I just wanted to say that I'm feeling really good and I'm feeling really strong and I'm feeling really... feeling. And that's something I haven't felt in a long time and I just want to say that I have all of you to thank for that...and myself. *(Bursts into tears.)* I'm sorry I didn't want to cry. *(Continues to cry.)* Thanks that's all sorry thanks.

RON: All right then thank you David.

JOE: Thanks David man.

TINA: Thanks David.

AL: Yeah thanks uh David.

RON: All right then anyone else like to share?

TINA: Yeah Ron. Hi I'm Tina and I'm cross-addicted.

RON: Hi Tina.

DAVID: *(Crying.)* Hi Tina.

JOE: Hi Tina man.

TINA: I'm not a man!

JOE: Hey sorry.

AL: Uh hi Tina.

TINA: Yeah right well I just want to say my effing mother's coming to visit me this week and she's staying in my effing bachelor apartment for four effing days and I am telling you that woman gets so on my effing tits I just want to go out and drink a silo of beer, I want to do an ocean of cocaine, I want to eat a swimming pool of donuts. I just want to go out and get so effing fucked up. But I'm not going to do that because that's why I'm here and other than that it's been a pretty good week and that's all and thanks for listening.

RON: All right then thank you Tina.

DAVID: *(Getting it together.)* Thanks Tina.

JOE: Tina.

AL: Yeah thanks Tina.

RON: All right then would anyone else like to share?…

AL: …Um. Well. Okay. Hi I'm Al. And I'm an… alcoholic.

RON: All right then Hi Al.

DAVID: *(Sniffling.)* Hi Al.

JOE: Hi Al.

TINA: Hi Al.

AL: Um. I just want to say that… What? Well. You people are pathetic. No I mean not pathetic I just mean I'm wasting my time. Or your time I mean. Sorry. I mean because this is silly I mean not silly but serious, it's me who—uh yeah so that's all. Thanks.

RON: All right then thanks Al.

JOE: Thanks Al.

DAVID: Thanks Al.

TINA: You fuc—

RON: All right then we'll adjourn the meeting. Keep coming back, it works.

            (Light shift.)

ADAM: That poor bastard.

            (Sound: "Hi Adam.")

ADAM: Fuck off this isn't about me this is about Al. That poor bastard. He's trying so hard—that's what he'd say "I'm trying so hard." But I mean you look at him and what do you see: a guy who can't help alienating everyone every time he opens his mouth, he hates his job, he has no friends, he's mean to his girlfriend and doesn't respect her enough to leave her. But underneath it all Al's special. Of course aren't we all. But Al's especially special because I chose Al to be part of my story. I wonder what he's thinking? Right now.

            (Light shift.)

AL: I am such an idiot. "You people are pathetic." Why can't I just keep my mouth shut? Obviously I have no ego. How could I possibly have an ego and still humiliate myself like that in public. Can a person live without an ego? If I could just blame someone but who am I going to blame? My father? That's such a cliche. I could though I mean he is a walking talking breathing argument for mandatory sterilization. Or I could blame my mother but that would be unfair since she's seventy-five. "Seventy-four!" Seventy-four whatever Mother for Christ's sake does it really matter! I mean I know I was abused I just can't remember it. If only I could find the right therapist I'm sure I could remember it in one session. But I was neglected that's for sure—Christ until I was seven I thought my name was Rob Roy. Maybe I just need to develop a sense of humour. God how much longer am I going to have to live this miserable life?

(Black out.)

JANINE: Who are you talking to?

(Light.)

AL: Nobody, myself, nobody.

JANINE: How was your day?

AL: Great.

JANINE: Are you being sarcastic?

AL: Oh Janine, I used to feel like I felt everything and now I feel I feel like I feel nothing.

JANINE: Oh honey, how was your meeting?

AL: Oh I don't think it's for me.

JANINE: Well you've only gone three times.

AL: Yeah but I don't think I fit in.

JANINE: You think too much. Gimme a kiss.

AL: *(Kiss.)*

JANINE: How do I look?

AL: Good.

JANINE: "Good."

AL: You do look good. I thought we were just going to a movie.

JANINE: I'm allowed to look good to go to a movie.

AL: Yeah.

JANINE: Guess what.

AL: What?

JANINE: I'm ovulating.

AL: Oh God Janine…

JANINE: We talked about it.

AL: I know but …

JANINE: You said when you got back on your feet.

AL: But I'm not on my feet. I'm barely standing.

JANINE: But you're headed in the right direction and nine months from now you're going to be fantastic.

AL: Ohhhhh…

JANINE: Shall we go?

AL: …Sure.

JANINE: Why are you bringing your briefcase?

AL: I'm going to stay at my place tonight.

JANINE: Okay I'll get my toothbrush.

AL: *(Sigh.)*

JANINE: You don't want me to?

AL: No sure that's good.

JANINE: You know we should talk about moving in together soon.

AL: Yeah. We can talk about it.

JANINE: Once we get married.

AL: *(Sigh.)*

JANINE: I'm old-fashioned. I don't know why people are so afraid of commitment. You have to be strong to know how strong you can be.

AL: Right.

JANINE: You just don't believe you deserve to be happy.

AL: Don't Janine.

JANINE: You don't want to get married?

AL: Not tonight.

JANINE: You don't want to get married tonight or tonight you don't want to get married?

AL: Do we have to talk about this right now?

JANINE: No we don't.

          (Pause. JANINE hums "Raindrops Keep Falling on My Head.")

          What are you thinking?

AL: I'm thinking I'm not talking.

JANINE: I know. But what are you thinking about that you're not talking about?

AL: I'm not talking about the fact that I'm not thinking about anything.

JANINE: Oh.

          (Pause.)

          So what movie are we seeing?

AL: Uh I forget what it's called a guy from group was talking about it. Yasmine Bleeth is in it.

JANINE: Who?

AL: I don't know. It's a love story.

JANINE: Oh a love story.

AL: Um hm.

JANINE: So. You don't want to have this baby?

AL: This baby? Which baby?

JANINE: The baby I want to have.

AL: Are you pregnant?

JANINE: Noooo.

AL: Then why do you keep talking about it?

JANINE: I'm ovulating I can't help it.

AL: Look, I don't know.

JANINE: Or is it that you don't want to have a baby with me?

AL: No. It's just I… I really don't think I'd make a very good father.

JANINE: You'd make a wonderful father.

AL: What makes you think I would make a wonderful father?

JANINE: Because you're so sensitive.

AL: I'm not sensitive Janine I'm depressed. Plus I have no ego.

JANINE: You have an ego. You have a wonderful ego. You are the king of your world, you line your fears up against the wall and call the firing squad.

AL: What have you been reading?

JANINE: I don't know. That just came to me. But it's good.

AL: Yeah yeah—look I just don't think I have anything to offer a child—I feel empty enough as it is. I think I'd just end up resenting the kid because it had a life.

JANINE: Don't be ridiculous—you have lots to offer a child. Love for example. There are so many unloved children in the world.

AL: Exactly! There are too many children in the world already.

JANINE: Al. I don't want to get political. I want one of my own.

AL: Your own! You can't own a child Janine!

JANINE: That's not what I mean. Please Al... I have half a baby in here right now all I need is a little help from you.

AL: I don't know what you want me to do other than to sacrifice myself for your happiness.

JANINE: Well why not. That's what I do for you. That's why they call it a relationship.

AL: Oh come on.

JANINE: Oh come on what?

AL: Listen to yourself, you're playing the martyr again.

JANINE: No I'm not Al.

AL: And you're suffocating me to boot.

JANINE: Al don't be mean.

AL: You harpie!

JANINE: Al!

AL: Harpie harpie harpie!

JANINE: Al!

AL: Harpie harpie harpie!

ADAM: Now now you two shut up I'm trying to watch the movie.

(Light shift.

JANINE watches the movie and becomes slowly horrified.

JANINE rushes out.)

JANINE: I can't believe you took me to see a movie like that in my condition.

AL: What condition?

JANINE: I'm ovulating. My egg is probably traumatized.

AL: Your egg's not traumatized.

JANINE: Oh thank you Doctor, tell me more about my womb.

AL: I'm sorry I didn't know it was going to be like that.

JANINE: That was so disgusting—the idea that a child could do that to his parent. Why would anyone make a movie like that?

AL: Oh Janine wake up, read the papers, it happens.

JANINE: Oh stop it. I'm going to have to get DNA tests now, all my eggs are probably traumatized.

AL: Don't be stupid.

JANINE: You took me to that movie to hurt me.

AL: I wasn't thinking of you.

JANINE: Exactly!

AL: Get off my back!

JANINE: I know what your nightmare's about Al—it's about the fact that you're a selfish S.O.B.

AL: Oh fuck off.

JANINE: *(Gasp.)* I beg your pardon?

AL: I said "OH. FUCK. OFF."

JANINE: No. You, fuck, off.

AL: No you fuck off.

JANINE: No you fuck off.

AL &
JANINE: *(Together.)* No you fuck off!

ADAM: No you fuck off!!

(Sound: "Hi Adam.")

ADAM: Fuck off. Damn. Huh? Damn. Those two. You can almost smell the wedding cake but they just can't seem to see eye to eye. Well it looks like the only thing to do is to pack it in, to roll the credits, to clean the slate. But some people just don't know when to stop. See for some people life is like a bad haircut: at first you think: "How am I going to live with THIS!" but enough people remind you that it will grow out and eventually it does and then before you know it there you are: back in the same barber's chair. You see what a person needs at a time like this is good advice but you can't get good advice from just anybody and unfortunately when the chips are down some people will talk to just anybody. Won't they Al?

(Light shift.)

AL: *(Driving.)* I am so angry. I am so mad. I am so angry at you. I don't even know why I'm talking to you, why do I bother. I just want to break something or hurt someone or hurt myself just to spite you—but I haven't got the heart. I want to go out and get absolutely shitfaced drunk...and don't try and tell me what to do don't—as if you would anyway—you never have before why start now all I ever get from you is the same useless shit over and over—I am so tired and so angry and just so finished so finished so finished with you. *(Honk.)* Crazy kids.

(Pause.) And could you please make Janine come
back. Ow! And could you please make this not be a
kidney stone.
Amen.

(Light shift.)

ADAM: Oh yeah some people will talk to anybody when
the chips are down. Won't they? Don't they? Don't
you?
What do you want? What do you really want? "I
want peace in my home. I want to raise my children
well. And I want to get off occasionally." No no
what do you really want? Under that. Come on.
What do you really want? The respect of strangers?
More money for more stuff? Sex on demand? No
no no what do you really want? Come on. Proof
that she loves you? Assurance he'll stay? No.
Under that. What makes the world go round? Yes.
That's it. You're not such an asshole after all. What
do you really want? Revenge. Revenge. For
everything. Revenge. For having been born into
this shithole. Revenge. REVENGE!

(Light shift.)

JERRY
BUSTER
FOSTER: Hello. Hello. I'm Jerry Foster. Jerry Buster Foster.
Perhaps you've heard of me, I'm a former
filmmaker. Ah perhaps you haven't, I'm about as
former as you can get. I'm thinking I should change
my name to Jerry Buster Former. I don't normally
come out in public like this these days—but I was
disturbed by something I'd been hearing about
and I thought I'd better say something about it—if
for nothing else but my own peace of mind. I
understand there's been quite a bit of talk about
this new film that's come out that is supposedly
based on my unfinished film *Hack* and I'd like to
say that this bothers me quite a bit—and it's

nothing to do with money or copyright or ownership or anything like that—you can't own an idea. But what it is about is why I didn't finish making the film in the first place. You see the idea came to me almost as a dream, one morning I woke up and there it was and I was a young man full of piss and vinegar and I'd had a bit of success so I just went ahead and started shooting. And I will say there were some wonderful things about the film: the opening scene with the darkness and the silence was lovely, and the scene with the highway and the river and the fish, well that was quite radical for the genre and Shelley Winters as the love interest—well...she was luminescent. But. The problem originated in the gruesome gruesome basement scenes with the father and the son and the hacksaw—and when I watched those scenes I was overcome by a deep sadness, because there was nothing there other than psychological cliche. And worse what was there was action motivated by nothing other than a desire to destroy and I'm sorry but that's not real. It's not real because its not human because we are creators not destroyers— and I know I know read the papers but I wonder if perhaps the evil that exists in the world today has to do with men like me making films like that. Isn't it just the exploitation of fear, the fear that is created by societal dysfunction which in itself is created, created by the institution's need to limit personal freedom in order to turn all thought into material consumption...or...well, once a Marxist. But the point is I stopped making the film and not finishing the film effectively destroyed my career as a filmmaker. But I felt very strongly then—as I do now about this new film—that we don't need to show that sort of thing. What we need to do, and if ever there was a time in the world it is now, is to turn our attention away from the darkness away from this thing we seem to have made. We must take that responsibility. I can't imagine it's too late.

So I would like to ask each of you now, in your own way, to turn your attention away from the darkness and toward the good things. Toward the …the…the… Shu… Shu… Shu…

(Light shift.)

ADAM: Shut up!
It was real. It was so real. Action motivated by desire to destroy—you love that stuff. You're suckers for it. It appeals to your dark side. I think it's a fine film and if you don't that just proves what a pretentious cretin you are. Asshole. Yes I'm talking to you. Are you offended? You should be because that's my job. I insult you so you can feel indignant. I humiliate you so you can feel justified in your self mutilation. I make you feel bad about yourself so you can in turn condescend to the peons you surround yourself with. I am your anger and your resentment. I am your boredom and your restlessness. I am your apathy and your self consciousness. I am that part of you that would rather see the man drown, rather see the forest fire, rather see the dam break, rather see the darkness win. I live in this world as a virus. In this world that you created. In this world that needs to know, know, know all the dirty details so it can be as smart, smart, smart as it can be. And where does smart get you? Standing at the edge of a highway, ready to take that step, hoping for a miracle.

(Sound: "Hi Adam.")

Hi.
Think of me whenever you read about those terrible things in the papers that remind you how low you can go, how strange it can get—how there is no logical explanation—no answer to… "why…" —Remember me when you sense the eternal darkness all around you, when you feel the inescapable darkness in your heart.

Shh! The movie's sta…ah…ah…ah…

(Light shift.)

JANINE: *(Laughing.)* Well I'll tell you something about that movie, I'm glad Al and I went to see it, because if we hadn't we wouln't have fought and if we hadn't fought we wouldn't have made up and if we hadn't made up I might not be pregnant now. I'm so happy. This is what I've always wanted. And Al and I are going to get married, as soon as his kidney stone clears up. Just a small wedding. And I sure won't be wearing white. I guess I'm a little old-fashioned and a little modern at the same time. But I guess you have to be, it's a new world. Al's a little worried but that's all right he's a bit of a worrier.

This baby is going to be so happy. This baby is going to be so loved. This baby is going to be someone special. We've already found out its going to be a boy. Al will be a wonderful father. He'll teach him to play ball and to fish and how to ride a bike. I can't wait to tell the whole world. "Al and Janine Boyle proudly announce the birth of their son—Adam." How's that for a little hope at the end of the day.

(JANINE turns into ADAM.)

ADAM: *(Yawning.)* Good night. Sleep well.

(Music and light to end.)